Dropping In On...
CHINA

David C. King

A Geography Series

ROURKE BOOK COMPANY, INC.
VERO BEACH, FLORIDA 32964

A Blackbirch Graphics book.
Series Editor: Tanya Lee Stone

Printed in the United States of America.

Library of Congress Cataloging-in-Publication Data

King, David C.
    China / by David C. King.
        p.   cm. — (Dropping in on)
    Includes bibliographic references and index.
    ISBN 1-55916-087-X
    1. China—Juvenile literature. 2. China—Description and travel—Juvenile literature.   I. Title. II. Series.
    DS706.K55   1995
    951—dc20   94-39643
                                              CIP
                                              AC

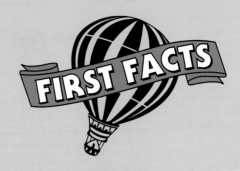

China

Official Name: People's Republic of China

Area: 3,696,100 square miles

Population: 1,192,000,000 (1 billion, 192 million)

Capital: Beijing

Largest City: Shanghai (7,500,000)

Highest Elevation: Minya Konka (24,900 feet)

Official Languages: Chinese and Mandarin

Major Religions: Officially Atheism; traditionally, Confucianism, Taoism, and Buddhism

Money: Yuan

Form of Government: Communist Party-led state

Flag:

TABLE OF CONTENTS

 OUR BLUE BALL—
THE EARTH
Page 5

 THE NORTHERN
HEMISPHERE
Pages 6–7

 GET READY FOR
CHINA
Pages 8–9

 STOP 1:
SHANGHAI
Pages 10–11

 STOP 2:
NANJING
Pages 12–13

 STOP 3:
CANTON
Pages 14–15

 THE FAMOUS
FOODS OF CHINA
Pages 16–17

 STOP 4:
CHENGDU
Pages 18–19

 LIFE IN A
YUNNAN
VILLAGE
Pages 20–21

 STOP 5:
TURPAN
Pages 22–23

 STOP 6:
DONGXIANG
Pages 24–25

 GROWING UP
IN CHINA
Pages 26–27

 STOP 7:
BEIJING
Pages 28–29

 THE GREAT
WALL
Page 30

 GLOSSARY
Page 31

 FURTHER
READING
Page 31

 INDEX
Page 32

Our Blue Ball—The Earth

The Earth can be divided into two hemispheres. The word hemisphere means "half a ball"—in this case, the ball is the Earth.

The equator is an imaginary line that runs around the middle of the Earth. It separates the Northern Hemisphere from the Southern Hemisphere. North America— where Canada, the United States, and Mexico are located—is in the Northern Hemisphere.

The Northern Hemisphere

When the North Pole is tilted toward the sun, the sun's most powerful rays strike the northern half of the Earth and less sunshine hits the Southern Hemisphere. That is when people in the Northern Hemisphere enjoy summer. When

the North Pole is tilted away from the sun, and the Southern Hemisphere receives the most sunshine, the seasons reverse. Then winter comes to the Northern Hemisphere. Seasons in the Northern Hemisphere and the Southern Hemisphere are always opposite.

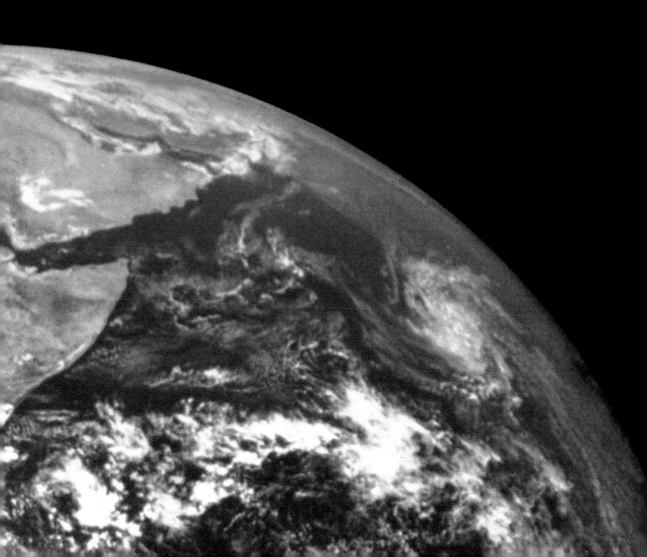

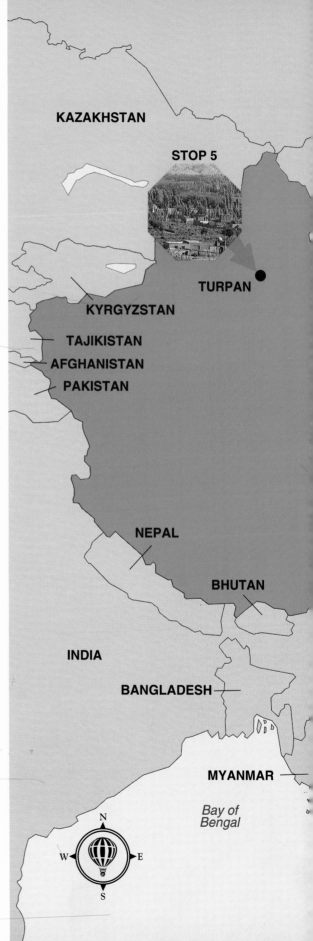

Get Ready for China

Hop into your hot-air balloon. Let's take a trip! You are about to drop in on a country that is about the same size as the United States. One special fact about China is that it has many more people than any other country in the world.

China is located in the Northern Hemisphere on the continent of Asia. On the east, it is bordered by the Yellow Sea, the East China Sea, and the South China Sea. Farther east is the Pacific Ocean. Some of the highest mountains in the world are located along China's southern border.

KAZAKHSTAN

STOP 5

TURPAN

KYRGYZSTAN

TAJIKISTAN

AFGHANISTAN

PAKISTAN

NEPAL

BHUTAN

INDIA

BANGLADESH

MYANMAR

Bay of Bengal

N
W   E
S

RUSSIA

Lake Baikal

MONGOLIA

STOP 6

STOP 7

BEIJING ⭐

DONGXIANG

NORTH
KOREA

*Yellow
Sea*

SOUTH
KOREA

JAPAN

STOP 4

STOP 2

NANJING

STOP 1

SHANGHAI

CHENGDU

Yangzi River

STOP 3

*East China
Sea*

TAIWAN

CANTON

Hong Kong
(U.K.)

VIETNAM

LAOS

HAINAN

*South China
Sea*

THE PHILIPPINES

THAILAND

CAMBODIA

China

⭐ National Capital

0   500 Miles

Stop 1: Shanghai

Our first stop will be the city of Shanghai (Shang·hi), on China's east coast. Shanghai is one of the largest and most crowded cities in the world. More than 7 million people live in the city.

The Yangzi (Yang·tshee) River flows into the Sea of Shanghai. The Yangzi is one of the longest rivers in the world. It winds its way through China for nearly 4,000 miles. The river and the sea make Shanghai the busiest seaport in China.

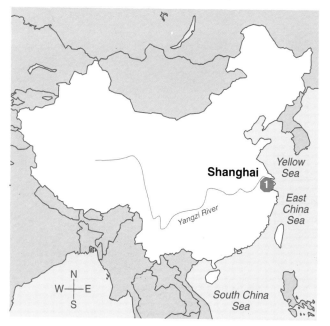

Shanghai is an old city, but it also has modern stores and towering office buildings. The shopping areas glitter with neon signs. A beautiful park called the Bund stretches along the riverfront.

Opposite: Cruise ships and other boats fill Shanghai's seaport.

Next, let's travel **northwest** along the Yangzi River to the city of Nanjing.

Inset: Every morning in the Bund, people perform an exercise called taiji (tie·gee).

Stop 2: Nanjing

Nanjing (Nan·jing) is a large city that is on the southern bank of the Yangzi River. There are many factories in the city. Some are well known for clothing and other items made of silk.

Nanjing is a very old city. As you walk along the streets, you can see parts of the ancient city wall. The wall was built more than 700 years ago.

Another famous site is the Grand Canal. It is the largest human-made waterway in the world. You can take a cruise on the Grand Canal in a boat called a *junk (junk)* or in a smaller boat called a *sampan (sam·pan)*. Along the way, you will see fields of rice and wheat. Some people wash their clothes in the canal and others fish from its banks.

A busy street in downtown Nanjing has both old and new buildings.

Now we'll travel **southwest** *to the city of Canton..*

A Chinese junk glides
through the water at sunset.

Nanjing ②-① Yellow
Sea

East
China
Sea

Yangzi River

South China
Sea

N
W—E
S

Stop 3: Canton

The city of Canton (Can·tahn) is in southern China, on the banks of the Pearl River. Like all of China's cities, Canton mixes the very old with the new. Modern hotels, office buildings, and stores line the riverfront. The city is known for its many ancient Taoist and Buddhist temples. The temples, called pagodas, have several stories, each with a separate roof that curves upward.

Canton is known for its handmade crafts, especially carvings of ivory or jade. Most of all, the city is famous for its food. You might try a meal of sharks' fin soup, rice, crispy chicken, and steamed vegetables. There are also other unique dishes, such as dried squid and stewed fish heads!

This pagoda in Canton is called the Six Banyan Temple.
Opposite: People enjoy wandering through this busy Canton neighborhood.

The Famous Foods of China

Four different regions of China are famous for their foods. The foods of the Canton region are probably best known because they are served in Chinese restaurants all over the world.

Northwest of Canton, in Sichuan (Se·shwan) Province, the cooking is very different. Sichuan food is usually very hot and spicy. One Sichuan dish is *mapo doufu (ma·paw doe·foo)*. Tiny pieces of pork and bean curd are cooked in a thick, spicy sauce with garlic and onions. Frogs' legs, smoked duck, and dried chili beef are other favorites. The sauces are so hot, you will need plenty of rice and tea to stop the burning in your mouth.

In the far north of China, it is too cold to grow rice. Instead of rice, the cooking in this region uses noodles or dumplings made of wheat flour. One special food in this region is Beijing (Bay·jing) duck, served with pancakes and plum sauce. Many of the northern dishes are stir-fried or barbecued.

The fourth region of great Chinese cooking is the area around Shanghai. Shanghai cooking uses lots of shrimp and fish. Other favorite dishes are ham-and-melon soup, and drunken chicken, which is soaked in wine.

China is known for the variety of delicious foods made in each region of the country.

From Canton, we'll travel **northwest** to Chengdu.

Stop 4: Chengdu

A Giant Panda sits in a field eating bamboo.

The capital of Sichuan Province is Chengdu (Cheng·doo). It is a crowded, noisy city with many shops and factories. Along the tree-lined streets, you can watch rows of tailors running their sewing machines with lightning speed. Street vendors sell flowers, vegetables, and baskets.

In the afternoon, many people head to one of Chengdu's famous teahouses. Each teahouse offers some special entertainment. In some, people play chess or a game called *go*. In other teahouses, you can listen to a musician or a storyteller.

The area around Chengdu has many farms. You can see rice paddies or fields of wheat. The fields are separated by mulberry trees or groves of bamboo. China's silkworms live in mulberry trees.

Mountains rise to the west of the city. The Giant Pandas live in the bamboo forests on the mountain slopes. They are endangered animals. The people of Sichuan Province are working hard to protect the remaining pandas.

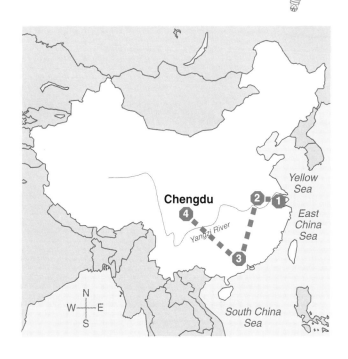

People gather for an afternoon break in a teahouse.

Life in a Yunnan Village

China has many large cities, but most people live in small towns or villages. In Yunnan (Yun·nan) Province, more than 25 million people live in scattered villages.

The Yunnan region has the nicest weather in all of China. Summers are warm and dry, and winters are mild.

Villagers on their way to market cross a small bridge in Yunnan Province.

The farm families of Yunnan grow wheat and rice. After the wheat crop is harvested, the fields are plowed again and then flooded. Rice is then planted in the shallow water of the flooded fields.

Market days and festivals are exciting. Markets are held out of doors, with tables piled high with food and other goods. Festivals are held to celebrate many holidays.

*Next, we'll travel **northwest** 1,000 miles to the town of Turpan*

Stop 5: Turpan

We are now in Xinjiang (Sing·kee·yang) Province, in the far northwest corner of China. This is a rugged land of mountains and deserts. Winters are very cold and summers are the hottest in China.

The Turpan oasis lies at the base of the Flaming Mountains.
Inset: A Uigur couple stops working to pose for a picture.

In the north of the province is a low area called the Turpan (Tur·pan) Basin. It is the second-lowest spot in the world. In the center of the basin is the town of Turpan. Turpan is an oasis—an area in a desert that has water from underground streams. Open channels carry the water to people's homes and to farm fields where wheat and vegetables are grown.

The people of Turpan are not Chinese—they are called Uigurs (You·gers). The Uigur people have lived on this oasis for many centuries. Their religion is Islam, so there are several mosques in the town.

The town is small, with only a few main streets. You will see people traveling to their farm fields in donkey carts. Beyond the oasis are the Flaming Mountains. In the afternoon sun, the mountains look as red as fire.

Now let's head **southeast** to the town of Dongxiang.

Stop 6: Dongxiang

The town of Dongxiang (Dong·shang) is located in a region called Inner Mongolia. This is a huge area of grassland in the far north. Summers here are mild, but icy winds sweep across the region in winter.

Many of the people in the area of Dongxiang are Mongolians. The grasslands are perfect for raising horses, cattle, sheep, goats, and camels. For many centuries, the Mongolians have lived as nomads—people who move often from place to place. Today, many live in towns like Dongxiang. But others remain nomads, moving their herds and flocks from one grazing area to another.

Left: These shepherds can construct their yurt in several hours.

These hardy shepherds build special homes called *yurts* (*yöt*). A *yurt* is a dome-shaped tent. The frame is made of willow branches bent to meet in the middle. Layers of cowhide and felt are then stretched over the frame. A hole in the center of the roof, called a *toono* (*too·no*), lets light in and smoke out. The *yurt* can be taken down and folded up for travel.

In the summer, the Mongolians hold a festival called Naadam. There are horse and camel races, and archery contests, with prizes for the winners.

Below: Everyone attends the annual Nadaam festival to join in the fun.

LET'S TAKE TIME OUT

Growing Up in China

Children in China go to school 6 days a week. In most parts of the country, the school day begins at 7:00 A.M. and ends at 3:30 P.M. In many schools, the day starts with breakfast and then morning exercises.

Students spend a lot of their time learning the Chinese language. Chinese is a difficult language because it has so many different characters. While the English alphabet has 26 letters, or characters, Chinese has thousands. By the time they are 10 or 11, students will know almost 3,000 characters. Students who go to college will learn 5,000 more.

Schoolchildren also study history, science, math, and music. In most schools, students begin learning English when they are 7 or 8 years old.

Families in China are very close. Kids help with the housework and take care of younger brothers or sisters. Children are taught to obey all older family members, including aunts, uncles, grandparents, and older brothers and sisters.

Opposite: Chinese schoolchildren wave a friendly greeting.

For our final stop, we'll travel **northeast** *to Beijing, the capital of China.*

Stop 7: Beijing

China's capital is a large city of nearly 6 million people. The city has many wide streets lined with trees. There are also many large public squares. One popular place for tourists to visit is Tiananmen Square. Tiananmen means "Heavenly Peace."

Another famous spot in Beijing is called the Forbidden City. This is where the emperors of China once lived. For more than 500 years, only royalty was allowed to enter this large area of palaces. Today, it is a museum open to the public.

The Forbidden City is surrounded by thick walls and a large moat. The moat has become a popular place for boating. Inside the walls, there are nearly 800 buildings.

Outside the walls of the Forbidden City, Beijing is very busy and crowded. Streets are clogged with cars, trucks, and bicycles.

Before we leave China, let's visit the Great Wall of China, near Beijing.

The people of China are now free to visit the Imperial Palace in the Forbidden City.

The Great Wall

More than 2,000 years ago, an emperor decided to build a wall to keep invading armies out of China. Later emperors added to the wall. In time, the Great Wall stretched for 4,000 miles.

Most of the wall is still standing, and thousands of tourists visit it each year. The Great Wall is made of mud, cement, rocks, and bricks. It stands 30 feet high, with watchtowers rising 10 feet higher. The Wall was made wide enough for 5 soldiers on horseback to travel side-by-side. In ancient times, signals were sent from one watchtower to the next. Smoke signals were used during the day and fires at night. The Great Wall is one of the only human-made structures that astronauts can see from space.

The Great Wall of China winds from the sea far into the center of China.

Now it's time to set sail for home. When you return, you can think back to your wonderful adventure in China.

Glossary

basin An area of the Earth's surface that is lower than land around it.

canal A waterway made by humans, large enough for boats or ships to pass through.

moat A channel of water built around a palace or castle for protection.

nomads A group or tribe that moves from place to place, rather than living in permanent homes.

oasis An area in a desert that has enough water for trees and crops to grow.

pagoda A temple or other building with several roofs that curve up at the tips.

Further Reading

Jacobsen, Karen. *China*. Chicago: Childrens Press, 1991.

Kalman, Bobbie. *China: The Land*. New York: Crabtree, 1989.

Kalman, Bobbie. *China: The Culture*. New York: Crabtree, 1989.

Murphy, Wendy. *Hong Kong*. Woodbridge, CT: Blackbirch Press, 1991.

Terzi, Marinella. *The Chinese Empire*. Chicago: Childrens Press, 1992.

Index

Beijing, 28–29
Beijing duck, 16
Bund, 10, 11

Canton, 14–15, 16
Chengdu, 18–19
Chinese food, 16–17

Dongxiang, 24–25

Flaming Mountains, 23
Forbidden City, 28, 29

Giant Panda, 18, 19
Go, 18
Grand Canal, 12
Great Wall, 30

Imperial Palace, 29

Junk, 12, 13

Mapo doufo, 16
Mongolians, 24–25

Naadam, 25

Nanjing, 12–13
Northern Hemisphere, 5, 6–7, 8

Pagoda, 14
Pearl River, 14

Sampan, 12
Shanghai, 10–11, 16
Sichuan Province, 16, 18, 19
Six Banyan Temple, 14
Southern Hemisphere, 5, 6, 7

Taiji, 11
Teahouse, 18, 19
Tiananmen Square, 28
Toono, 25
Turpan, 22–23

Uigurs, 22

Xinjiang Province, 22

Yangzi River, 10, 12
Yunnan Province, 20–21
Yurt, 25

Acknowledgments and Photo Credits

Cover and pages 20–21: ©J. Aberham/Leo de Wys, Inc.; pp. 4, 6–7: National Aeronautics and Space Administration; p. 11: ©W. Hille/Leo de Wys, Inc.; p. 11 (inset): ©Jerry Cooke/Photo Researchers, Inc.; pp. 12–13: ©Carroll Seghers II/Photo Researchers, Inc.; pp. 12 (inset), 14, 19, 30: China National Tourist Office; pp. 15, 22 (inset): ©Noboru Komine/Photo Researchers, Inc.; p. 17: ©Mike Wilson/Leo de Wys, Inc.; p. 18: ©Okapia/Photo Researchers, Inc.; pp. 24–25: ©P. Koch/Photo Researchers, Inc.; p. 24: ©Joan Lebold Cohen/Photo Researchers, Inc.; p. 26: ©Stan Ries/Leo de Wys, Inc.; p. 29: ©Steve Vidler/Leo de Wys, Inc.

Maps by Blackbirch Graphics, Inc.